PRAISE FOR YOUR VOLUNTEERS

"Healthy churches understand the importance of building and empowering volunteers. *Your Volunteers* provides simple, proven strategies to help you grow volunteer engagement. No matter what size your church, you need the insights found in this book."

— Tony Morgan, author, consultant, leadership coach
(TonyMorganLive.com)

"No one has shaped our discipleship systems of volunteerism and small groups more than Chris Mavity. This work will prove to be simple, practical and biblical."

— Shawn Lovejoy, Directional Leader, Mountain Lake Church
and Churchplanters.com; author of *The Measure
of Our Success: An Impassioned Plea to Pastors*

"Thank goodness someone finally wrote this book. I wish I could have read it 20 years ago. Chris Mavity not only recaptures the power of the priesthood of all believers, but has given us the roadmap for calling, equipping, empowering, and unleashing the greatest asset in every church."

— Gene Appel, Senior Pastor,
Eastside Christian Church,
Anaheim, CA

"This is a manifesto on volunteers. I v
with whom I consult to make this book
entire staff."

— Dick Hardy,

D1059441

www.thehardygroup.org)

"Over the past 10 years, Chris Mavity has added more value to my thinking on volunteer ministry than anyone. The most impressive part of Chris's leadership in this area is that the volunteers he leads stay for life! I know because I've met some of them. Reading this book will save you years of painful trial and error. Read this now."

—CASEY GRAHAM, Founder,
The Rocket Company

"Mobilizing volunteers is a big challenge for the church today. Getting the right people with the right gift mix into the right spot serving joyfully—that is the goal. I don't know of anyone who is more qualified to speak on that than Chris Mavity. It's what he has been doing at North Coast for years! Read this book and get his insights on how you can do this at your church. Then just follow his methodology—you'll thank me later!"

—JIM SHEPPARD, Generis, Principal & CEO;
co-author of *Contagious Generosity*

"Chris Mavity writes from real life experience. Chris's passion and personal example has literally changed our ministry. Our small group ministry went from struggling to survive with a handful of groups to thriving with over 60 groups within a couple of years. None of that would have been possible without his practical advice on volunteer ministry. This book will help you too."

—JOSH HAWLEY, Pastor of Spiritual Growth,
The Bridge Church, Fresno, CA

"Chris Mavity has an uncanny knack for identifying and trouble-shooting the most common and often the most resilient challenge that exists in any organization—namely, volunteerism. Having had the privilege of knowing and learning from Chris over the years, it is hard to believe that this book is his first one. This book is a quick page-turner as it is filled with so many practical ideas you can implement right away. In fact, you'll want to implement them without delay if you are serious about transforming the volunteer culture of your organization."

—K. J. AHN, Assistant Pastor,
Open Door Presbyterian Church,
Herndon, VA

"Volunteers are the life blood of every church yet too often they are seen only as a means to get things done. Chris Mavity knows from experience that as go your volunteers, so goes your church. I have had the privilege to experience the results of his philosophies and leadership as I have been served by the volunteer army at North Coast Church. I have seen no finer group of servant-minded people in my life! It therefore is no surprise that North Coast is a thriving, healthy church. For that, and many other reasons, I am thrilled that Chris has decided to share his thoughts in *Your Volunteers*. I know you will be challenged and encouraged by the wisdom Chris shares. You will also walk away with practical tools to implement a revolutionary approach to volunteers in *your* church!"

—STEVE CATON, Leadership Team,
Church Community Builder,
Colorado Springs, CO

your
VOLUNTEERS

your VOLUNTEERS

FROM COME-AND-SEE
TO COME-AND-SERVE

Chris Mavity

This work is dedicated to:

Pete and Janet Helland
David and Loretta Nelms
Lewis and Leah Nelms
Larry and Nancy Osborne
Thank you for your investment in Kathy and me.
We are better because of you.

CONTENTS

ACKNOWLEDGMENTS

People who have invested in us over the years are vast in number, patient in outlook, and diverse in background. To those who've trained us, helped us, and nurtured us along the way (whether you knew it or not), thank you.

There are thousands of volunteers who have said yes to a ministry call under my watch. They are the foundation of the words that follow. To each of you: Keep the faith and thank you for your trust.

To the elders, pastors, ministry leaders, and volunteers at North Coast Church: Your camaraderie and care are very much appreciated, and your example serves the kingdom well.

To those pastors and leaders from churches around the country with whom I've been privileged to engage: Thank you. You've impacted my life and ministry greatly!

your VOLUNTEERS

FOREWORD

Chris Mavity has a heart of gold and a genuine heartbeat for people that God gives to the church. But that's not why you should read this book.

Chris is a master teacher and an experienced practitioner in one of the most effective church models of our day, but that's not why you should read this book.

So why read this book? In answering this question, Steve Jobs comes to mind. Years ago, with the debut of the iPad, Jobs gave us something we didn't know we needed. Now, people everywhere, engage their digital worlds with beauty and ease that they didn't know was possible.

Chris has done the same. Now pastors and church staff everywhere can move into their volunteer worlds with beauty and ease that they didn't know was possible.

Your Volunteers provides transferable insight that is just amazing. You will quickly wonder how you did ministry without this profoundly practical guidance. For example, consider:

- Are you aware of how "training" is different from "equipping?"
- Do you know the three things every volunteer wants?
- Would you like to have a memorable road map for dealing with difficult volunteers?

At one point while reading this book, I found myself a bit uptight that someone had not provided teaching like this earlier in my ministry!

As you engage *Your Volunteers*, I trust that you will be as grateful for Chris Mavity as I am. He has taken the time to share both his genuine passion and his break-through wisdom so that you and *your volunteers* might win for the mission of Jesus.

—WILL MANCINI
FOUNDER OF AUXANO, author of *Church Unique*

INTRODUCTION

When you look out upon the vast landscape of ministry, what do you see? What draws your immediate attention? Particular programs, complex processes, overwhelming needs, significant opportunity? Perhaps you are drawn to all the tasks, troubles, and timelines that ministry today seems to require. To be sure, it's all there, and no matter the size of your ministry there's a lot of it! In fact, there is so much that no one person—despite his or her talents, gifts, abilities, or anointing—can get it all done.

Early in His ministry, Jesus recognized the simple fact that He couldn't do it all and that He'd need help. Jesus' solution? Volunteers.

That's right. Jesus selected volunteers to join His ministry effort. Today, we call twelve of Jesus' early volunteers *apostles*. We read about their selection and training in the Gospels, and their ministry results are outlined in the first part of the book of Acts and various New Testament epistles.

Ministry strategy hasn't changed much over the past couple millennia. Today, there is still too much to do but not enough time to do it, and no one person possesses the talents, gifts, abilities, and anointing to do it all. Your solution? Volunteers!

YOUR GREATEST MINISTRY ASSET

There is one resource every church has more than anything else: people. Churches (with few exceptions) have more people than money, space, or staff. That means to be effective, we must have a good game plan in place for helping those who *come and see* to become people who *come and serve*. By having an effective game plan, we increase our potential to grow and have positive impact on our congregation, our community, and beyond.

Let's consider the sports and business worlds. The most successful sports teams and businesses thrive with an effective game plan centered on having the right people in key positions. This is a vital element to their success.

Ministry strategy hasn't changed much over the past couple millennia. Today, there is still too much to do but not enough time to do it.

Sports teams hire talent scouts to scour small town ball fields, and college and minor league teams look everywhere for talented players who can help their team win. Corporations hire headhunters to search the heights and depths of the talent pool to find just the right person for a specific role. These organizations are willing to invest significant resources of time, effort, energy, and money to locate and hire the right people because, over the long haul, their return on that investment proves more than worth it.

What would happen if we took a similar approach toward volunteers in our church? What if we started to see the people in our church as our greatest asset? Not only worth the investment but, in fact, the very reason to invest. What if our approach to volunteers was as intentional and integral as finding the right player for a sports team or the best leader for a business? And why not? It is the kingdom after all!

When we as pastors and church leaders shift our mindset and see our volunteers as true disciples and adjust our practices to reflect that importance accordingly, the trajectory of our ministry makes an immediate upward tilt. It takes that type of mindset to develop a thriving group of volunteers who serve with passion and love what they do and who they do it for.

What results is the foundation of a thriving volunteer ministry. The following five benefits are in store for you and your ministry as you adopt the principles and practices outlined in this book and thus create your own thriving volunteer ministry:

1. *Expand your foundation.* No church can grow beyond the strength of its foundation. Nor can it afford to hire all the help necessary to skillfully serve the congregation and community in which it resides.

2. *Create momentum.* Thriving volunteers attract more volunteers. People talk to other people. They share about their experiences. They encourage others to do what they love doing. Think about it: word of mouth can be a great ministry tool when working with volunteers.

3. *Lighten the load.* As more people engage in ministry, more work gets done—but it can also be easier to do. Two horses pulling one wagon can haul a lot more than each horse individually.

4. *Foster longevity.* Volunteers who are fulfilled in their roles keep serving even when ministry becomes challenging. When you match people to roles uniquely suited for their divine makeup, skill set, personality, and interests, you produce volunteers who last.

5. *Create buzz.* Visitors are impacted by the volunteers you have in place. First-time guests at your church will typically encounter a number of volunteers on any given

week, and those volunteers often become some of the greatest points of connection for new attenders.

These certainly aren't the only benefits of a church with a thriving volunteer ministry, but these are some big wins your church can experience when it has thriving volunteers serving.

So how do we lead in such a way that those who *come and see* become those who *come and serve*? There are two components necessary to accomplish what I call a thriving volunteer ministry: environment and operations.

> *So how do we lead in such a way that those who* come and see *become those who* come and serve?

The environment is what people sense about the physical, spiritual, and emotional vibe of your place. Thriving environments are healthy, vibrant, and attractive. Operations are comprised of five fundamental skills deployed within the environment to produce a specific result. It is the combination of, and interplay between, your ministry environment and your ministry operations that will work in synergy to create a thriving volunteer ministry.

Both environment and operations matter and are equally important. We'll begin with a look at environment in Part One, and then we'll unpack the operational skills necessary for effectiveness in your volunteer ministry in Part Two.

Part One

YOUR VOLUNTEER ENVIRONMENT

All ministry happens within a particular context. The broad context of ministry is what I'm referring to as the environment. Your church has one . . . is it the environment you want?

Environment matters. In fact, environment impacts all of us whether we realize it or not. Think about the environment of different climates such as the Amazon rain forest or the Sahara Desert: Life exists in both but is radically varied in each place. The requirements necessary for abundant life to exist in these two environments are literally a world apart.

Another great metaphor for understanding a ministry environment is farming. For a farmer to be successful and have a crop at harvest time, a lot of work needs to be done in the winter, spring, and summer. The winter is spent planning, getting equipment ready, and determining what crops are planted in each field. Spring arrives and all hands are busy preparing the soil and planting the precious seeds. The summer is spent tending the field, weeding, watering, and inspecting the crops. Finally, fall comes and with it the harvest.

However, the harvest is only as bountiful as the environment allows. If you have a great environment, you'll likely have a great harvest. I have a saying: "There are no corn fields in Alaska."

"That's a dumb saying," you might conclude. "Of course there aren't any cornfields in Alaska. The environment isn't conducive to growing corn!"

Well, sometimes we try to accomplish the ministry equivalent of growing corn in Alaska. Just as corn grows much better in Iowa where the environment is conducive to a bumper crop, volunteers thrive when conditions surrounding them are favorable for ministry and in an environment that is designed to maximize their gifts.

So what can we conclude when it comes to creating a thriving environment for our volunteers? Environment is made up of the conditions surrounding the volunteer: the physical, relational, spiritual, and operational conditions. With the right environmental elements present, you have set the stage for a thriving ministry to volunteers.

I grew up in the Midwest, the agricultural breadbasket of America. If you wanted to earn some cash in the summer you went to work for a farmer. Back then, I didn't appreciate the lessons I was learning while at work in the fields. It just seemed like a lot of hard work to get a little extra spending money. What I learned, however, was that there are three environmental factors that influenced the size of the harvest: soil, sunlight, and rain. These three elements correlate with the three areas that demand our attention when it comes to creating a ministry environment where volunteers can thrive: value, energy, and alignment. These are the soil, sunlight, and rain of volunteer ministry.

Farmers spend a lot of time preparing the soil with fertilizer, adding nutrients so that in the fall they will have a robust harvest. They are adding value to the soil. The sunlight provides the energy required for the seed to grow and develop into a plant. The rainclouds provide water that allows the seed to germinate and ultimately produce a crop.

Soil, sunlight, and rain create an environment for growth in the fields; likewise, value, energy, and alignment create an environment for growth and healthy development of our volunteers. Let's explore each of these in turn in the chapters ahead.

Chapter One

VALUE: YOU KNOW IT WHEN YOU SEE IT

V alue is the soil of our volunteer environment. Without healthy soil, our volunteers will not feel valued, nor will they live up to their potential. So how do we value our volunteers? How do we ensure our volunteer environment communicates that we need and value the people who have committed to come and serve?

Value, to our volunteers, begins with *acceptance*. First, we must accept them for who they are: the sum total of their past, present, and future. That's easy enough, you might conclude. But let me point out that there is a difference between *accepting* a person and *tolerating* them.

Accepting someone means you meet them where they are without taking on the responsibility to change them. I know, I know. This is ministry. Aren't we as spiritual leaders supposed

> *Accepting someone means you meet them where they are without taking on the responsibility to change them.*

to change people? No, not really—that is the Holy Spirit's responsibility. Our responsibility is to work to create the environment conducive to the change that may need to occur.

Tolerance, on the other hand, means that I'll hang out with you and be around you as long as I can see that you are moldable and adaptable to my preferences or ways of thinking or behaving. The bottom line is this: acceptance leaves the work of molding and shaping a person up to the Holy Spirit whereas tolerance puts me in charge.

People know when they are accepted rather than tolerated—just as you do. When you accept others, they feel more valued so they give more value in return.

Second, value is demonstrated when someone is *authentically known*. To know someone authentically means that you go beyond acquaintance or familiarity. You come to know more than just the logistics of their life such as where they live, where they work, or how many kids they have. When you know someone authentically you understand what makes them tick: their personality, their preferences (likes and dislikes), their prickle points (you can raise their ire with just a phrase or two), and their positions (you know where they stand on issues and what's most important to them). When you know and understand someone at that level—beyond the small talk—they feel valued.

Third, value is shown when you *appreciate* someone for who they are and what they do. Appreciation is likely the greatest unused commodity in volunteer ministry. I know we can get busy juggling balls and spinning plates like a circus clown, which leaves little time for small things like a simple "thank you." But these small things are important. They compile over time to make a real and lasting difference in the lives of those we lead. Appreciation is the *currency* of volunteer ministry.

Appreciation in its best form is both *personal* and *specific*. The more personal and specific the appreciation, the greater value is shown. There's no need to drain the budget with galas and gifts when a heartfelt thank you that is personal and specific will do.

"Ben is a good guy" is an opinion, but it doesn't demonstrate true appreciation because it is neither personal nor specific. "Ben, you're a good guy" is better since it is personal (spoken directly to Ben), but it still isn't specific. (What does "good guy" mean, anyway?) "Ben, thank you for serving on the parking team. You not only help folks find a parking spot, you make people feel welcome at church even before they get out of their car." It's very likely that Ben would feel more valued by the last comment than either of the first two.

VALUE ENHANCERS

Once you begin to create value—step one in creating a thriving environment—you can further enhance the value you bring to your volunteers by practicing the following:

Listen Well

Listening seems to be an art form of the past. In today's noisy world, everyone wants to shout loud enough to be heard. The listening leader will add value and therefore become more valuable. If listening were a stock on the New York Stock Exchange ("LSTN") its value would be soaring today.

Limit Surprises

Surprises startle people, and startled people don't do much more than discuss what startled them. Startle them enough and they'll develop a nervous tic and eventually quit. Over the years, I've been amazed at what has been accomplished by our ministry teams because we informed them ahead of time and minimized—or better yet, eliminated—unwelcome surprises.

Provide Honest Input and Feedback

Volunteers appreciate honest input and feedback from their leaders. For many volunteers, ministry is a risky proposition, and of course they want to do well. Giving them honest input and feedback rids them of uncertainty and helps settle any anxiety.

I love Jesus' example (recorded in Luke 10) when He sends out the disciples two by two. He instructs them, sends them off, and when they report back He gives them honest input. It made the disciples better and more useful for the work at hand. The right people will value honest input and feedback given at appropriate times and in appropriate doses.

Move Toward Problems

We know that there are plenty of problems that come our way in ministry. They may be unavoidable, but they are not *unsolvable*. If we ignore, cover up, or dismiss problems as no big deal, value diminishes quickly. A wise leader tackles problems up front and moves toward solutions.

YOU NEED VOLUNTEERS— VOLUNTEERS NEED YOU

There is still a lot about volunteer ministry to cover, but I think value is the right place to begin. Ministry involves people—human beings. People have feelings, hopes, and dreams. A good habit to build into relationships, especially with the people who matter to you, is to find a way to value them.

You'll be amazed how fast a culture that values volunteers will transform your church. We'll never get the chance to lead anyone—especially volunteers—until we are able to accept them, authentically know them, and appreciate them. It seems so simple, but far too few leaders work toward this on a regular, systematic basis.

Creating a thriving volunteer ministry is not a far-fetched fantasy; it's something you can experience in your church. It all begins by adding value—the foundation stone to help create a thriving environment.

Chapter One in Review

Key Ideas

1. Valuing your volunteers begins with accepting them.

2. Valuing your volunteers is demonstrated when you seek to truly know your volunteers.

3. Valuing your volunteers is shown by expressing personal and specific appreciation.

4. Seek to listen well, provide input and feedback, and move toward problems to show that you value your volunteers.

Discussion Questions

1. Which of the three elements of Value is most challenging to you: accepting people as they are, seeking to know them, or expressing appreciation?

2. What are three things you can do in the next quarter to show your appreciation to your volunteers?

3. Rate your performance in each of the Value Enhancers (Listen Well, Limit Surprises, Provide Honest Input and Feedback, and Move Toward Problems). Which are you doing well? Which one needs work? What can you do differently?

4. What challenges you about God's plan to use people to bring His vision for your church? How can you move forward in seeing people as God does?

Chapter Two

ENERGY: NOT MUCH HAPPENS WITHOUT IT

I t takes a measurable amount of energy to accomplish anything worthwhile. Ministry is no exception. Energy is needed to get things moving and keep things in motion. As leaders are well aware, energy isn't permanent. It gets used up and must be replenished.

One of the primary jobs of a ministry leader is the creation, allocation, and conservation of energy. Leading volunteers requires spiritual, emotional, physical, and mental energy . . . and a lot of each!

CREATING ENERGY

The single most effective way to create energy is to win. From little leagues to major leagues, winning creates energy. Consider what happens when little Johnny's team wins its game: The team and its fans in the bleachers get an immediate dose of energy. Everyone is exuberant. The same is true at the professional level. The more important the game, the more the win adds energy. Although it takes a lot of energy to win, the win always produces more energy than it took to achieve.

Conversely, in a loss, energy is sucked up like a chocolate malt through a straw! As excited as Johnny's team is from the win, the losing team is equally saddened, despondent, and defeated. Both teams expend energy during the game, but the winning team gets it all back—and then some—because winning creates energy.

> The single most effective way to create energy is to win. From little leagues to major leagues, winning creates energy.

Your volunteers need to know what winning looks like in your ministry; and you must tell them. That way, when they achieve a win in ministry, they'll celebrate and be reenergized. If we fail to identify and acknowledge the win for our volunteers, those serving on our ministry team may lose sight of the end game. They will toil, serve, and work hard, but to what end? If the wins are never acknowledged, despondency and a forlorn attitude begin to set in. Though they undoubtedly have the big picture of God's kingdom in mind, we've got to make them aware of—and initiate the celebrations for—the everyday ministry wins.

By the way, scores lead to wins. Scoring during the game creates energy as well. The rule of thumb is this: Applaud the scores (Johnny's base hit) and celebrate the victories (when the team wins the game).

Scoring and winning aren't the only ways to create energy with your volunteers. We help create energy when we invest in people. Training—helping our volunteers become better—is a sure way to increase energy. (We'll discuss this further in Chapter Five).

Time and shared experiences—simply hanging out and having fun together—is a big energy boost.

Rewards and awards also help create energy. I'm sure you've seen it or experienced it yourself. Rewards for a job well done make a person want to continue to do the job well (and even improve). I experienced this as a young man in a retail management position. The owner of the company decided to reward certain behaviors. The result was that profit margins climbed and the staff made some extra money. Then out of the blue the rewards were removed—but the expectation was to continue the previously rewarded behavior. I'll bet you can guess what happened. You got it: everyone went back to the old behaviors because the lost reward was seen as a slight. Profits plummeted and the speed at which our company lost energy (and the momentum it created) was astounding.

Another way to create energy is to match the right person with the right job. If someone enjoys a job and is good at it, satisfaction ensues, which increases energy. Your call as a volunteer leader is to assess the volunteers in your midst, know their gifts and talents, and then allocate their skills to the proper need.

Placing volunteers properly takes some energy, to be sure. But it will give a greater return on energy because people will be working in roles that energize them and build excitement within the group. (We'll discuss placement of volunteer leaders more in Chapter Six.)

ENERGY FUELS YOUR VOLUNTEER MINISTRY

Energy is so vital to a thriving volunteer environment that we must take action when a volunteer simply isn't working out. The leader must protect the energy at all costs. It's simply too hard to come by to allow someone (or something) to rob the energy from those who are making ministry happen. There are some volunteers who, quite frankly, drain energy. It's like they pulled the plug in the bathtub: The energy spirals down the drain and, quicker than you thought possible, the tub is empty. What can you do to conserve energy when faced with that situation?

I call that energy-robbing volunteer a *NAG*. They are easily identified because they are continually *negative, arrogant,* or *grumpy* (or a combination of the three). Left unchecked, NAGs can consume so much energy that others will mock them, avoid them, quit the team . . . or worse, become NAGs themselves.

What is the solution to a NAG?

NAG them back.

No, you don't become like them! Let me explain. The appropriate treatment of a NAG is to *neutralize* them, *advise* them, and *give them specific options*.

First of all, attempt to *neutralize* a NAG. Limit their exposure and influence on other volunteers by reassigning them or positioning them in a role so that their behavior is of little to no effect upon others, thereby neutralizing their unwanted influence.

If that isn't possible (or doesn't work) the next step is to *advise* them. Have a private conversation with a NAG, being honest with them about how their attitude or behavior is affecting others on the team. It's important to make it clear that continuing the unacceptable behavior is not an option. The objective here is to help people overcome the issue, difficulty, or trouble they are experiencing. If your advice is followed, you've just had a big win (thus creating energy). Advising NAGs takes an investment on your part. These individuals may require added training, continuing conversations, or even a good old "come to Jesus" meeting. But the investment is usually worth the effort. Whether or not your advice is heeded, rest assured the conversation must be had or you will begin to lose other valuable members of the team.

Finally, as a last resort, if you are unable to neutralize or advise a NAG successfully, then you must *give them specific options*. As best you can, help them understand that the mission is most important and that, for now, they must:

- Comply to the ministry standard(s)
- Correct unwanted behavior, or
- Give up their ministry role

Creating, allocating, and conserving energy so it can be released intentionally is a must for a leader to enjoy a thriving volunteer ministry. When you infuse energy into your volunteer environment, it will spread to your volunteers throughout your programs and add vitality to your vision. By utilizing these ideas, you can create, allocate, conserve, and release the energy needed to get things moving—and keep them moving—for the good of the kingdom and your volunteers.

Chapter Two in Review

Key Ideas

1. A thriving volunteer ministry runs on energy.

2. Energy is created through ministry scores and wins, community building, and the proper use of rewards and awards.

3. Energy is too important to allow a NAG to waste it.

Discussion Questions

1. On a scale of 1 to 10 (1 being the least amount of energy and 10 being an extreme amount of energy), what is the current energy level of your volunteer ministry right now? Why?

2. How are you creating energy within your volunteer leaders today?

3. In what ways are the placement of volunteers and the attitude of volunteers connected? Which volunteers display the highest amounts of energy? Why?

4. Do you have a plan to deal with volunteers who don't bring a lot of energy to their work? Recall one experience where you had to deal with a NAG. What did you learn?

Chapter Three

ALIGNMENT:
WORKING IN UNISON

H ave you ever driven a car that was out of alignment? It's a constant struggle to keep the car on track (not to mention it's a bit
dangerous). Sure, the car can get you to the destination and
back again, but it is hard to control, energy is wasted, and the tires
wear out quickly.

That's the way it is in ministry when we're not in alignment. Ministry works but it is unstable; it wastes time, effort, and energy; and
we wear out people instead of tires.

THE WHAT, WHY, AND HOW OF ALIGNMENT

Your ministry is aligned when your volunteers understand *what* you
are trying to accomplish, *why* it's important to accomplish it, and
how we plan to accomplish it.

It's important to be aligned to principles rather than to processes, programs, or people because principles endure while
processes, programs, and people are temporary. Keep in mind that
the principles to which you are aligned will shape your ministry. For
example, a small group ministry aligned to evangelism will function

27

differently than one aligned to inductive Bible study. A worship ministry aligned to service will look different than one aligned to performance. A hospitality ministry aligned to greeting will interact differently than one aligned to welcoming.

When all involved in a particular ministry endeavor gain a clear understanding of the what, why, and how, energy is used effectively and the intent is almost certainly accomplished. We have a much higher likelihood of making the difference we are all working toward.

There are a few side benefits of alignment worth mentioning.

Alignment allows for quick yeses. There will no longer be a need for drawn-out meetings and ongoing debates that delay our ability to take action.

Alignment also allows for graceful nos. If you cannot say no in ministry, you'll likely burn out. If you are unable to say no gracefully, you'll likely get put out.

Alignment helps us gain confidence. Even the newest volunteers gain confidence when they know what they are doing, why it is important, and how to get it done. Confidence without alignment is difficult for even the most seasoned ministry veteran.

Alignment allows for longevity. It's tough to last anywhere if you are zigzagging in ministry. Alignment keeps the ministry on the right track over the long haul.

FINDING ALIGNMENT

How do you find alignment? Over the years, I have had the privilege of helping hundreds of church teams work through a process of determining their ministry purpose and direction. The core of this exercise can be very challenging but extremely helpful to gain clarity and ultimately work toward greater alignment in ministry. You can help your own ministry and your volunteers serving in your ministry teams by honestly answering the following five questions:

1. Who am I really?
2. Where have I been?
3. What have I done?
4. Where am I now?
5. What do I want?

This may seem like a simple exercise—it's only five questions. I've learned, however, the answers aren't necessarily quick or easy, nor are the results automatic. These questions and the answers to them are not a magic pill or ministry fairy dust. Utilizing these questions regularly and repeatedly over time will help you produce the alignment that both you and your volunteers need. Having greater clarity regarding who you are and where you and your ministry are going will help simplify and streamline your ability to develop thriving volunteer teams in your church.

Here's a hot tip: the process of grappling with the questions—not necessarily your answers to them—is the win. It's the experience of working *through* this process that will help you gain great clarity and develop alignment in your ministry. I first answered these questions over ten years ago. I'm now in the habit of answering them on a monthly basis. It helps me stay aligned both personally and professionally.

ALIGNMENT'S POWER

The power of alignment is unmistakable in ministry. Everyone notices its impact. When alignment is achieved, the right people do the right things at the right time in the right way. Everyone wins. When alignment is missing, things can still work out, but the negative effects such as burnout, tension, conflict, frustration, and indifference exact a toll on everyone involved.

(Note: Alignment is a big component in creating a thriving

volunteer environment. For more on alignment read *The Unity Factor* and *Sticky Teams* by Larry Osborne. He is the best directional leader I know.)

THREE THINGS EVERY VOLUNTEER WANTS

For the most part, I believe the people who make up our volunteer teams want the same basic things out of life that you and I do. In fact, I believe every person in every church wants to say the same thing about his or her church experience: it is fun, fruitful, and fulfilling. And whether or not we use the same expression or phrase, the reality is that when something isn't fun, fruitful, and fulfilling, we will eventually stop doing it.

Your volunteers want to be part of something that is:

1. *Fun.* People enjoy doing things that are fun with people who are fun; they avoid things and people that aren't. That doesn't mean everything in church ministry has to be a party, but it does mean volunteers who stay involved in ministry will find roles they enjoy first and foremost. Thankfully, not everyone enjoys the same thing.

2. *Fruitful.* There is a great deal of satisfaction that comes from seeing results. Diet and exercise products on TV show us that. A result offers credibility and affirms that the product, program, or process works. The same is true for your volunteer teams. When they experience progress or see results, it affirms the work and sacrifice they have invested has had a payoff.

3. *Fulfilling.* Life is too short to spend our days doing things that don't connect with the core of who we are. Even

things that are fun and fruitful are tainted if they aren't also fulfilling. It's important that volunteers experience fulfillment and satisfaction in the roles they fill and areas of ministry in which they serve.

> It's important that volunteers experience fulfillment and satisfaction in the roles they fill and areas of ministry in which they serve.

If you find your work with volunteers fun, fruitful, and fulfilling, then it likely will be for them as well. The leader who understands these three principles and applies them to his or her leadership of volunteers will most likely have volunteers who experience these qualities as well.

ALIGNMENT STABILIZES YOUR VOLUNTEER MINISTRY

Finding and maintaining alignment is crucial to a thriving volunteer ministry. Without it, your ministry will be unstable, often veering off in the wrong direction. Proper alignment ensures that you aren't wasting time, effort, and energy on activities or people that don't match your mission. And best of all, alignment makes sure volunteers aren't getting worn out due to confusion and inefficiency.

Alignment joins *value* and *energy* as the three core elements that produce a thriving volunteer ministry environment. Together, these three factors provide the result you and your volunteers dream of—greater kingdom impact. But having the perfect environment isn't enough; you still must operate within the environment you've helped to create. We'll address the critical operations component of your thriving volunteer ministry next.

Chapter Three in Review

Key Ideas

1. Alignment defines the what, why, and how of your volunteer ministry.

2. Be sure to align volunteer ministry to principles (timeless) rather than processes, programs, or people (temporary).

3. Having greater clarity regarding who you are and where you and your ministry are going will help simplify and streamline your ability to develop thriving volunteer teams in your church.

4. Volunteers align to ministries that are fun, fruitful, and fulfilling.

Discussion Questions

1. Take time to define the what, why, and how of your volunteer ministry.

2. What timeless principles do you want your ministry aligned to?

3. How would you answer the five alignment questions for your ministry? (To keep in alignment, mark your calendar to revisit these questions regularly in the year ahead.)

   - Who am I really?

   - Where have I been?

   - What have I done?

   - Where am I now?

   - What do I want?

4. What makes your ministry fun? Is your ministry aligned so that your volunteers find it a fruitful use of time? What makes your volunteer ministry most fulfilling to your volunteers?

Part Two

YOUR VOLUNTEER OPERATIONS

Let's say a farmer has the environment working in his favor: perfect soil, plenty of sunlight, and the right amount of rain. Those very necessary and good things don't guarantee a bumper crop. There's a lot of work yet to be done in the field. How the farmer operates with all his tools and equipment will have a dramatic impact on the size of the upcoming harvest.

Likewise, just because you have an environment that has healthy and vibrant doses of value, energy, and alignment doesn't mean you'll have thriving volunteers. You must also operate effectively.

There are five operational skills necessary to capitalize on that healthy environment in order to produce a thriving volunteer ministry. The five operational skills work in synergy with one another and in concert with environment to create the thriving, robust ministry we all want.

The five operational skills you'll need to employ to develop thriving volunteers are:

1. *Recruit:* Ask and select well
2. *Train:* Invest first

3. *Place:* Match people and positions

4. *Support:* Be there when it matters

5. *Monitor:* Evaluate for effectiveness

Let's explore each of these in more detail (see the appendix for the Synergy Diagram).

RECRUIT: ASK AND SELECT WELL

E ven the healthiest of volunteer environments won't produce a thriving ministry if there are no people willing to serve as volunteers. Every volunteer ministry needs a system for recruiting people to move from a come-and-see mentality to a come-and-serve mindset. You have the great responsibility of finding the right people to serve in the right role for the good of the kingdom.

One of the great privileges we have as leaders in God's church is that we get to help people discover their role in the kingdom and activate them to work for eternal things. I can think of few things more satisfying than watching people grow in their faith through volunteer experiences.

RECRUITING STRATEGIES

The two most common recruitment modalities we employ in ministry today are: to *fill a slot* (the most common) and to *select a person*.

Each modality is useful and necessary. When we need a lot of people who we can train quickly to do a specific assignment on a temporary basis, it would be wasteful to have them interviewed, fill out assessments, and run them through various approval channels. Conversely, when we are faced with needing specific and specialized talent, experience, or giftedness, it would be best to take more time and energy to find the right person for the job.

The reason both recruiting strategies are needed is because not all volunteers are created equal. Generally they fit into one of three categories.

1. *Hobbyist.* These volunteers approach ministry as something good. They're interested in it, they are available, they get the job done, they get benefit from it, and they enjoy it—but they're not necessarily highly committed or interested in increasing their capacity or capability.

2. *Apprentice.* The second type of volunteer acts and behaves more like an apprentice, someone who has a certain level of skill or giftedness useful in ministry and wants to develop it further. They invest the time, effort, and energy necessary to get better, and their results show promise.

3. *Craftsman.* This final type of volunteer has honed and developed specific ministry skills that are necessary and, if missing, the ministry would suffer. These individuals are pillars of the church and often are involved in developing others for future ministry needs. A telltale sign of a craftsman is that they think about ministry even when not engaged in ministry activity.

For roles and positions that are short term and have less influence, it's fine to fill a slot. There are benefits in doing that because you can get a larger number of people involved quickly. This allows you to see how they act, how they behave, what they're good at, and what they like and don't like doing. Then you can help them adjust to find a different area of ministry if they desire a better fit as time progresses.

When you fill a slot, *the job gets done*. And that's about it. But there is a benefit to getting the job done! There are a lot of jobs that need to be done in ministry.

There are ministry positions where it's important to select the right person who has a specific skill set—such as a singer or a worship leader. Not just anyone can fulfill the role of being on a worship team! They need to be able to carry a tune and keep a beat. You don't want just anyone doing that. You can't just fill a slot; you have to select the right person.

In those cases, when we select the right person for the right job, *the mission gets done*. So it is important for you to spend your recruiting efforts in both categories, filling slots and selecting people. If you only concentrate on filling open slots in ministry, you will constantly be filling slots. You will operate only within the tyranny of the urgent. However, when you select people that have the talents, skills, gifts, abilities, and anointing for specific roles within your church, then you complete the mission of the church rather than just completing a series of tasks.

RECRUITING METHODS MATTER

Remember that both recruiting methods are useful and necessary. Both are needed within your church. Different people will respond to different approaches. It's not likely that an apprentice type volunteer is going to respond to an "all call" recruitment effort. It's just as unlikely that a hobbyist volunteer will respond well to the type of role and commitment that a craftsman would enjoy.

While necessary and somewhat useful, using the "all call" approach for volunteers places us at the most elementary level of kingdom engagement. Its intention is to fill slots for a specific event or a role, but it often offers only a temporary fix to a systemic volunteer issue.

Mass recruiting strategies may work well for an event or a one-time engagement, but for more permanent ministry endeavors it leads to a never-ending battle of tracking people down, playing the "guilt card," and hoping someone will just stick to whatever random role they were recruited for so the process doesn't need to be repeated all over again. Alas, that never works for more advanced ministry roles— the kind that help us fulfill the mission versus simply get a job done.

Now we're going to focus on "select a person" as a recruiting method because the all-call approach is already well understood and employed by most churches.

SELECT THE PERSON: RECRUIT FROM A POSITION OF STRENGTH

Selecting the right people is necessary for moving your mission forward, but few leaders are sure about how to do it. Here is the four-step process for selecting the right volunteer:

1. Know What You Need

I can't emphasize enough how important it is to know the role you need to fill. What are the talents, skills, and abilities necessary to fulfill the basic requirements of the specific role? You don't need a spreadsheet; don't over complicate it—just keep it simple. For example, if you need a singer on a worship team, note that they can't be tone deaf. Or if you are looking for preschool volunteers, make sure they actually like working with children.

2. Know Who You Need

Identify the characteristics of the person ahead of time. Who you need is about characteristics versus skill set. Recognizing these in an individual and matching them up with a ministry role and responsibility is the magic of ministry. For example, a small group leader would need to possess a high social IQ. A greeter would need to be hospitable. This is where you might identify maturity measures that matter or any "nonnegotiables" for the role. I limit this to a maximum of three characteristics to avoid looking for a perfect miracle person who simply doesn't exist.

3. Ask for Them

Ask God. Pray for them. We are involved in a spiritual endeavor; involve the Spirit. I know this may seem trite and overused, but God wants to use volunteer roles to mold and shape us in His likeness. Serving others is a clear command in Scripture. Ask God to bring the right people.

Ask others. The more specific you can be about who and what you are looking for, the more successful you will be at finding the right person. Ask people you know and trust to think about people they know who fit the criteria you are looking for. For example, don't just ask for an usher; ask for someone who is engaging and personable. (As your church grows, creating a referral engine will be very important because you won't know every church member.)

> *The more specific you can be about who and what you are looking for, the more successful you will be at finding the right person*

Ask them. When you meet the right person, invite them to consider joining your team. Depending on the role, they might be able to start immediately or you may need some time to work through any requirements or role-specific training.

4. Develop a Process

Utilizing a selection *process* will outperform a selection *event* over time. You'll gain momentum quickly and enthusiastically as people are selected and placed in ministry effectively. A process is simply a series of steps that has a beginning, middle, and end. For recruiting, the beginning is how a person enters the process, the middle is how you explain the role and responsibility, and the end is simply an invitation to join your ministry team (if warranted). The great thing about a process is that it can be tweaked. You can make minor adjustments along the way so that the process matches your needs. Over time you'll refine your own process so it matches your style and fits the culture of your church.

Can you see the difference a selection process would bring to your volunteer recruiting efforts? It's very likely to be a game changer. Selecting people for ministry is all about connecting the right person with the right role at the right time. When we *select* people for ministry, we are helping them get activated in ministry areas where they are already gifted and anointed by God to do well.

Josh Hawley from The Bridge Church in Fresno, California, came to me when his church was revitalizing their small group ministry. Although they had some success in the past, the small group ministry had fallen behind and was at a low point. We outlined a plan to recruit leaders—specific leaders with specific skills.

Josh went to work, growing the number of groups from eleven to forty-three in about six and a half months. The process we developed together revitalized the small group ministry. This led to great success because Josh knew what he was looking for and therefore was able to connect quickly and easily with the right people who could do the job.

THE FUNCTION OF SPECIFIC
MINISTRY ASSIGNMENTS

As with every process—even one as successful as Josh's—you'll want to *clarify*, *refine*, and *simplify* how you select or recruit volunteers for

42

specific ministry assignments. Here's how those three principles will guide you as you build your base of volunteer leaders:

1. When we clarify *the what* and *the why* of the role, people know what to expect. People are busy, so they desperately need clarity regarding what you want them to do and why it is necessary. If you're not clear with people about what you need and why you need them, they won't be clear about how they can help. Clarity also allows people the confidence to say yes quickly when it is a good fit.

2. When we refine *the what*, we make room for growth. As you grow, your specific needs will change. You may need more of some roles, less of others, and likely a few new roles will be created in the process.

3. When we simplify *the how*, it is easier to accomplish missional outcomes and measure the effectiveness of our effort. We'll talk more about monitoring our success in developing volunteers in Chapter Eight. The bottom line is that simple things are more productive. And that's the point. We want to engage as many people as possible in ministry, so we can reach more people together.

Leslie Rowell from Tidal Creek Fellowship in Beaufort, South Carolina, used these principles to solve a problem they were facing in their volunteer base. The church was building a much larger facility, which would likely draw a lot more people . . . and require many more volunteers. Leslie realized that the volunteer foundation of her church was not solid; it lacked in purpose and direction.

She went to work determining *what* was important, *who* could do the job, and *how* to get it done. After clarifying that, she instituted a volunteer development program. That move helped lock in their current volunteers and made it easy for new people to understand quickly what they could do to help and how they would be fulfilled as a volunteer at Tidal Creek.

Bottom line: it worked even better than expected. Attendance is at an all-time high, and the enthusiasm and excitement (energy) that Leslie brought to the team has been invaluable in the development of Tidal Creek's ministries. By the way, Leslie was employed part time!

NO LIFETIME SENTENCES—PLEASE!

One objection I hear from time to time is that some people have been reluctant to accept a volunteer role because it's a lifetime sentence with no opt-out clause. Ironically, when folks have the freedom to opt out, they tend to last even longer because they are motivated internally to stay rather than feel forced to stay by someone else's expectations.

When you select people and ask them to serve in specific roles, be sure to establish a time commitment and an escape clause. This will set minds at ease and actually encourage people to get involved.

When you select people and ask them to serve in specific roles, be sure to establish a time commitment and an escape clause. This will set minds at ease and actually encourage people to get involved. You never know what frame of reference someone has based on past volunteer experiences. Without the specifics, a potential volunteer may assume the new assignment will be exactly like the old one—which could be reason enough to say no to joining your team.

A FINAL WORD ON RECRUITING

As already stated, getting to invite people to participate in ministry is one of the special things we get to do as ministry leaders. God didn't save people for them to sit and wait for His return. He wants his children to get involved. And it's the job of the ministry leader to help them to do so.

Taking a careful and calculated approach to selecting volunteers for specific ministry positions honors the ministry and elevates the significance of each and every volunteer. Ministry is for everyone; it's what we all are called to do. Recruiting is the means by which we select the *right person* for the *right role* at the *right time* in the *right place* in order to complete our mission, thus advancing the kingdom in meaningful ways.

Chapter Four in Review

Key Ideas

1. Use the fill-a-slot recruiting strategy when you have basic, temporary roles to fill.

2. Use the select-a-person recruiting strategy when you need a highly specified skill and long-term commitment.

3. Before you start selecting or recruiting anyone, identify the characteristics of the person you are looking for based on the roles you need filled.

4. When you select someone and ask him or her to serve in a specific role, be sure to establish a time commitment and an escape clause up front.

5. The most honoring thing we can do for others is to invite them to participate in local church ministry.

Discussion Questions

1. What is your current strategy for recruiting volunteers? How effective has that strategy been?

2. How well defined are the criteria by which you choose volunteer leaders? Do you have position descriptions and expectations in writing? How would that information help in the recruiting process?

3. What is the benefit of identifying the time commitment for volunteer positions?

4. What percentage of your congregation has received a personal, face-to-face invitation to participate in the ministry of the church?

Chapter Five

TRAIN: INVEST FIRST

O nce you have recruited someone—moving them from a come-and-see to a come-and-serve mindset—you'll need to train them to serve in their newfound ministry role. Although some leaders may assume that training is a list of dos and don'ts, I see training as the key to influencing future behavior. Training allows you to communicate expectations, prepare volunteers for service, and impart wisdom and know-how. Training is truly more important than many of us realize.

TRAINING VERSUS EQUIPPING

Sometimes the terms *training* and *equipping* are used interchangeably. I want to begin this chapter by making a distinction between them:

- *Training* is providing input, in various forms, to influence a person's future actions, attitudes, and behaviors. You'll need to train your volunteers so that they achieve the specific ministry outcomes you desire.

- *Equipping* is about providing the resources a person needs to perform the duties associated with the roles and responsibilities for which they have been selected. For example, a custodian needs a vacuum cleaner, a data entry volunteer needs a computer, and a Sunday school teacher needs a classroom and supplies.

With those differences in mind, we will focus on training volunteers to be able to step into the roles they are gifted for and called to do. We'll look at two different types of training: orientation training and ongoing training. Both are important, but they are approached very differently.

Orientation training helps your volunteers understand the role, responsibility, and expected outcomes of the assignment; the administrative processes of communication, problem solving, chain of command, boundaries, and budget; and, finally, the role-specific training necessary to fulfill the responsibilities of the position.

Ongoing training is broader and doesn't focus as much on skill set development as it does on life skill development. I know it sounds a bit backward. Hang with me . . . I'll explain orientation training first, then we'll take a look at ongoing training.

ORIENTATION TRAINING THAT WORKS

The objective in orientation training—for any role in the church—is to make sure the volunteer has the information necessary to become successful. They can't be successful yet, because they haven't begun.

I believe orientation training is the most important training that a ministry leader can conduct. Why? Because I remember when I first volunteered in ministry. I figured someone at the church had

50

made a big mistake when they asked me to help out. I knew my past, and I was aware that I knew nothing about the role in which I was about to engage.

I had sweaty palms and a nervous feeling in the pit of my stomach all because I had become a first-time volunteer. I'm glad I did it, though it would be so much better for volunteers if they could sidestep the inner turmoil I experienced.

When we take the time to orient our volunteers to the ministry role, they gain insight and confidence that will serve them well from the very beginning of their newfound role. We help them avoid much of the nerves and doubts of a first-time volunteer. Granted, we might not be able to completely rid them of the sweaty palms or anxious feelings, but we can at least minimize them. By the way, orientation training serves to *When we take the time to orient our volunteers to the ministry role, they gain insight and confidence that will serve them well from the very beginning of their newfound role.* strengthen and solidify your position as the ministry leader as well. That's a win—which creates more energy!

Keep in mind that the people you are training want to do the job. They volunteered to do it! They desire to do it well and are looking to you for guidance, information, and instruction in order to do so.

Your objective in developing good orientation training is to give the volunteer the minimum amount of guidance, information, and instruction necessary to complete the assignment well. No one expects to know every nuance of the position from the first day of orientation training. The truth is, most ministry training happens on the job. Your goal is to affirm your volunteers and help them gain confidence.

51

ONGOING TRAINING THAT WORKS

I've learned that once someone knows how to do the basics of their ministry role, trying to train them more or better is a lot like reteaching a child to ride a bike. Quite frankly, my kids didn't want (or need) me to teach them twice. Stepping into most ministry roles is a lot like riding a bike: although your first ride may be rather wobbly, you're good to go once you get it down.

I've found that ongoing training focused on life skills development is the most needed and the most well received by active volunteers. The most effective ongoing training is focused on helping your volunteers becoming a better *them*. Topics like decision making, parenting, group dynamics, communication, or conflict resolution have a broad application and make people better at being *people*.

I've also found that volunteers are excited to come to this type of training because it benefits them overall: at home, in their jobs, as community members, and so on. This type of ongoing training communicates that you care about them as people—not just in a ministry function at church—and that you are eager to invest in them to make them better in all aspects of their lives.

CHARACTERISTICS OF HEALTHY TRAINING

Healthy training programs are essential for a thriving volunteer ministry. There are plenty of training kits available on the market, but I would strongly encourage you to spend the time developing your own training material.

It's okay to borrow and learn from other leaders and churches, but don't expect a cookie-cutter program to work for you right out of the box. Take what you've gleaned and make it your own. When you make it your own you essentially train yourself. The better trainer you are, the better training you can provide for your volunteers.

As you develop your training, keep it:

> *It's okay to borrow and learn from other leaders and churches, but don't expect a cookie-cutter program to work for you right out of the box. Take what you've gleaned and make it your own.*

- *Simple.* Understand the purpose or scope of the meeting and center your information and activities on that single purpose. If you try to accomplish too much in one training meeting, you'll often miss the mark and the training will have no effect. If volunteers feel like you're wasting their time, they will be reluctant to show up at the next training opportunity.

- *Spreadable.* Volunteer training that works in one department of your church will likely be helpful in others (with a few modifications). There will certainly be specific circumstances or realities that are different but most training can be adapted and adopted.

- *Scalable.* As you grow, your processes will need to adjust to account for the number of volunteers you have. Early on you may be training one on one, then small groups of people, then larger groups. Keep in mind that most people prefer a small setting to a large one when it comes to training. For that reason, among others, your effectiveness is usually greater in smaller training settings.

- *Scrappable.* If something isn't working, scrap it. Just because it worked yesterday doesn't mean it is going to work today. Just because it doesn't work today doesn't necessarily mean it won't work tomorrow. Keep the focus on outcomes, engagement, participation, and—most important—productivity.

HONOR OR OBLIGATION?

Training your volunteers takes commitment, time, effort, and energy, and it's well worth it. In fact, the most valuable ministry asset your church has is its trained and equipped volunteer team. When you make a commitment to training your volunteers, you'll find:

1. *Volunteers are influential members of any congregation.* This is a group that has developed a sense of shared ownership. They are committed to the long-term success of the church's ministry and to kingdom things. I want to be around these people and available to them because these are the people who will expand my church's reach and capacity for ministry.

2. *Training keeps the focus on growth.* It's easy to get sidetracked dealing with only the problems and protocols of ministry. An ongoing training schedule puts important productive time in my schedule, helping me ensure active, productive volunteers.

3. *You can better anticipate what's next.* Ongoing training means I have to think further down the road than the people I'm training. Anticipating what's next is what leaders do. Get too wrapped up in the daily grind and you risk losing the time and energy necessary to understand where God wants you to lead your volunteers next.

> The most valuable ministry asset your church has is its trained and equipped volunteer team.

A passion for training volunteers will serve you well. These are the unsung heroes in ministry. You may not hit a grand slam every training session. Don't worry about it; that's not necessary anyway. They are your volunteers, and they want to hear from you. A commitment to ongoing training means that you'll get better, and so will your volunteers.

Training plays an important part in healthy volunteer operations. When you gather your volunteers together for orientation training or ongoing training, you have the awesome privilege of steering their thinking—and therefore the future behavior—of your entire team. Training puts the key ideas and character traits at the forefront, setting up your volunteers for ministry wins. (There's that energy thing again!)

Chapter Five in Review

Key Ideas

1. Training is about influencing the future actions, attitudes, and behaviors of your volunteers.

2. Orientation training prepares volunteers for service with the minimum details needed to perform their roles.

3. Ongoing training focuses on growing life skills and personal character.

4. A healthy approach to training volunteer leaders is to make it simple, spreadable, scalable, and scrappable.

5. Training is an opportunity to help prepare people for a spiritually formative experience God has planned for them through their volunteer ministries.

Discussion Questions

1. How often do you provide orientation training? What adjustments, if any, are needed in order to add volunteers to your team regularly?

2. How often do you provide ongoing training? What adjustments, if any, will ensure a valuable investment in your volunteers?

3. Review the healthy approach to training volunteers. How would you rate your training process in each of the following areas using a scale of 1 to 5 (with 1 being terrible and 5 being excellent): simplicity, spreadability, scalability, and scrappability?

4. What is the relationship between training and the spiritual vitality of your volunteers and church?

Chapter Six

PLACE: MATCH PEOPLE AND POSITIONS

H ow well do you know your volunteers? Do you know their God-given gifts, what they love to do, what hobbies they pursue and what they dream about? If you think about it, online companies like Google, Amazon, and Facebook (among lots of others) know a lot more about your volunteers' preferences than you do! How? Because they track online behavior.

If our ministry to volunteers is going to change in any significant way, we need to get to know *and* record their preferences, passions, personalities, and performance. Yet how do we get to know our volunteers? Can we do as well as those online groups do?

We certainly don't have the resources of a Google, Amazon, or Facebook at our disposal. Yet the only pathway to placing volunteers in roles for which they are gifted and anointed is by getting to know them. That's quite a challenge for a church of any size.

THE JIGSAW APPROACH

So, how do we get to know so many people at such different points in life? Let me share the quickest, simplest, and most effective method I'm aware of; maybe it'll work for you.

Have you ever attempted to complete a jigsaw puzzle? The box presents the picture on the outside. But when you take off the lid and look inside, you find hundreds (or thousands) of little pieces—what a complicated mess! But that mess, once properly connected, replicates the picture on the front of the box. Some puzzles are easy. Most are not.

People are incredibly complicated . . . It takes time and effort for a leader to put the pieces together and understand why a person is the way he or she is.

The same is true with a volunteer in your church. You've got a jigsaw puzzle with a grand picture on the outside, but inside there are hundreds (or thousands) of pieces that make up the complete picture of that person.

People are incredibly complicated—and often a bit of a mess. It takes time and effort for a leader to put the pieces together and understand why a person is the way he or she is. And that's for just one person.

How do we possibly manage such a feat for the entire church? "Impossible," you might conclude. You're probably right. You can't possibly spend every waking minute of every day putting together the jigsaw puzzle of each person in your church. It is important, however, to determine a manageable and reliable way to get to know those people God brings to you and your ministry. That's what we need to do if we are going to enjoy the success of a thriving volunteer ministry.

I haven't completed very many jigsaw puzzles, but I've started lots of them. I've also watched other people work on them as well. Whether a beginner or a veteran "jigsawer," they all start assembling the pieces just as I did. They identify the corners and edges as quickly as possible and put those pieces together first. In other words they work on the frame of the puzzle. The secret to placing people in ministry is identifying their four corners and their edges—the frame. That is typically done quickly, easily, and at little to no cost. Just about anyone can do it.

The key is looking at the placement of a volunteer the same way you'd start to assemble a jigsaw puzzle—by learning the basics about them (placing the corners and the edges). Then you will get a great sense of who the person is and go a long way to placing them in a ministry role where they can thrive. In time, through observation, feedback, and results, you will be able to place various inside pieces, allowing you to see and understand even more about the person. Here is what I've learned about this jigsaw placement process:

1. *I don't need to know everything about my volunteers.* In fact it's better to begin with the basics and add to your knowledge and awareness of them along the journey together. Many of the assessments, personality type indicators, and personal profile tools available today are intimidating from a potential volunteer's perspective, and they are often viewed as entirely impersonal. When you consider that many folks don't know themselves well enough to type out accurately anyway, the simplicity of a jigsaw construct may just be a better, more accurate starting point for you.

2. *I do need to know something.* You need to understand enough about people within the context of their relationship with the church (corners and edges) to make probable placements. The quickest way to determine their four corners is to learn what they value most. What is most important to them? This is most often revealed by how people spend their extra time and money—if they have any! Ask questions, then listen. You'll soon know what I call "the four corners" of the people you interact

61

with. If you understand what a person values in the world around him or her, you can make a very accurate initial placement decision.

3. *I need to record what I discover about people.* You're not going to remember all that you discover about people. Even if you could, others in your ministry don't have access to what you know. I strongly encourage you to find a record-keeping system that works for you. In today's social media, digital, fast-paced, information-overloaded world, it's becoming more and more important to know specific information versus only general information regarding those we lead and serve. Consider your church management system as an *investment in ministry* versus an *expense of ministry.* Utilize it to the fullest and you'll connect more people with more ministry more quickly and more easily than ever.

You might notice all these steps to knowing your volunteers are things *you* must do. It's up to you—and your ministry teams—to get to know your people by pursuing them (remember the parable of the lost sheep?). I know that when someone pursues me to learn about who I am and what I'm passionate about, I have a sense that they care. Your volunteers will feel the same when you seek them out.

RELATIONAL INTELLIGENCE TRUMPS STATIC ASSESSMENTS

Ministry flows from relationships, so let's relate with those we want in ministry.

Most volunteers don't want to complete a lengthy assessment, and it's worth mentioning again: many people aren't self-aware enough for an assessment to be a big help anyway. To make accurate connections between available roles and someone's interests, passions, gifting, and anointing takes someone who'll get to know that person, at least a little bit.

This is precisely why most direct appeals from the platform don't work for anything other than the most elementary volunteer positions. Placement isn't about staffing a production team of random people; it is about knowing enough about a person to pursue him or her and make a personal appeal with a customized opportunity to fit interests, skills, passions, and giftedness.

By the way, don't fret if it takes some time to complete the full puzzle of a person. Just be sure to capture the information you learn and then be consistent in recording it after your interactions with them. The jigsaw puzzle of "them" will begin to emerge. Also, be adaptive. As you learn more about your volunteers and have additional interactions with them, you'll find that your initial impressions weren't spot on. No problem. Just change a corner or two and some of the edge pieces to make it accurate.

There is nothing that makes volunteers feel more valued than when you understand who they are and that you're genuinely interested in helping them serve in roles that perfectly fit.

There is nothing that makes volunteers feel more valued than when you understand who they are and that you're genuinely interested in helping them serve in roles that perfectly fit how God has designed them.

As you place volunteers, you'll learn:

- *Good placement begins with active listening.* Listen for the cues people give about their hobbies, interests, experiences, skills, and backgrounds. As you do, you'll learn quickly where they'd like to participate in acts of service toward others.

- *Active listening begins and ends with questions.* To listen well (remember the stock symbol LSTN), make eye contact and don't talk. Ask open-ended questions that give space for people to reveal more about who they are. I'll also mention *don't interrupt* because I need to remind myself of that one.
- *Good questions lead to insightful conversations.* When you pick up on something someone says or does that is of particular meaning or interest, continue the dialogue around that subject.
- *Insightful conversations help you connect with people.* People may forget that they said hi to you in the hall between weekend services, but they won't forget if you took the time to talk with them about meaningful things. Most of us live busy lives. We rush to, from, and through church to get on with the rest of our day. When we genuinely connect with others, we create space for ministry placement opportunities and . . . *Viola!* Your empty roles get filled when you take time to talk with people.

PLACEMENT IS FOR NOW— NOT FOREVER

I've learned that ministry placement is often for a season, and as your volunteers mature and transition or as life happens, they may seek new or different opportunities. That's okay. Placement is an ongoing cycle, not a one-and-done task.

Placement is about getting the right person in the right place at the right time. But times change. In other words, how accurately does the jigsaw puzzle you started months or years ago match the picture on the box *today*? It all depends on how much of the picture you have put together at any point in time.

Matching the picture and the person is the secret to placement that leads to volunteers who have fun, are fulfilled, and experience fruit from their effort. It's not very likely that these volunteers are quitting anytime soon!

A few years ago, I met Mark, the senior pastor at Faith Community Church in San Diego. He was looking for some answers on moving ministry forward. He wanted his volunteers to see the overall vision of the church and how their roles fit into achieving it.

Upon some diagnostics and initial work together, it became clear that the church's communication of the vision needed clarification. Once people understood the vision, it was much easier to draw volunteers for specific missional assignments and then support them in a way that would make them volunteers for life—not necessarily doing the same role forever but by being committed enough to the overall vision to stay involved in ways that used their gifts to contribute to the success of the church.

Just one year later, Mark had a 100 percent retention rate of his new volunteers, and church growth was over 30 percent for the year. It all started with having an engaged and productive group of volunteers who were committed to the vision and to seeing positive fruit for the kingdom.

LEAD PEOPLE, MANAGE SYSTEMS

When we make the mistake of managing people and leading with systems, our goal is obvious to everyone: simply fill the openings with a warm body. "Who can help me now?" becomes the battle cry. If we do that long enough, we'll cry—because we end up with unfulfilled volunteers doing subpar ministry in a lackadaisical manner. Nobody wins in that scenario.

However, when we lead people and manage systems, we understand the profound effect that proper placement can have on the success and growth of any ministry. The wins rack up. As we've already learned, this is how *energy* and *momentum* are created—the two best friends of any leader!

Placement done well will require a bit more time and effort on the front end, but the payoff will be well worth it. Your constant attention and adjustment will be rewarded—so watch for how your volunteers grow and change over time, and keep your eyes and ears open for placing more pieces of the jigsaw puzzle that accurately depicts each one of your volunteers. You'll be glad that you did. (And so will they.)

Chapter Six in Review

Key Ideas

1. Google likely knows more about your volunteers' preferences than you do.

2. You need to understand enough about a person—the corners and edges of who they are—to make a suitable volunteer placement.

3. Volunteers feel most valued when you take time to understand who they are and when they know you are genuinely interested in helping them serve in a role that uniquely fits how God has designed them.

4. We should constantly look for opportunities to meet new people, maintain relationships, and find places where people fit in best to serve the kingdom through the local church.

Discussion Questions

1. Think about the volunteers in your area of ministry. What are some common characteristics of these people? What are some specific characteristics of key volunteer leaders?

2. What is your process for determining the suitability of a volunteer for an area of ministry?

3. How much of your time and resources do you invest getting to know new people, maintaining relationships, and finding ways for people to fit into the local church?

4. What are some steps you can take to improve your placing of volunteers?

Chapter Seven

SUPPORT: BE THERE WHEN IT MATTERS

A t some point, your volunteers will need support in order to experience success. None of us has everything it takes to succeed at everything all of the time. The manner in which you support your volunteers will contribute greatly to their overall success in ministry.

In fact, I would go so far as to say that an unsupported volunteer is a temporary volunteer. Support leads to success, which leads to longevity . . . and longevity leads to a healthy ministry. The goal of this chapter is to give you a framework for understanding support in the context of your volunteer ministry.

THREE TYPES OF SUPPORT

There are really three categories of support: proactive, reactive, and platforming.

Proactive support includes training, equipping, preparation, communication, and budget. Basically, it is laying the track on which to operate your ministry. *Reactive support* includes responding, fixing, clarifying, removing, feedback, and input. It means being available to help solve problems or issues. *Platform support* is the ultimate in support and is extended to proven volunteer leaders who merit a platform of their own. Let's look at each of these in detail.

Proactive Support: Equip and Train Volunteers to Do the Work

I mentioned in Chapter Five the difference between training and equipping. Equipping is making sure all the tools a volunteer needs to complete a task are ready, prepared, available, and in good working order.

As leaders, our job is to prepare everything volunteers need in advance of their time to volunteer. By serving your volunteers in this way, they are free to serve others. Training delivers the information and input they need so they can adjust their behaviors and/or develop the character necessary to become maturing, effective servants. Both are forms of proactive support.

Support means helping your volunteers when you are needed and standing back when you aren't.

Anything done to support the ministry efforts of the volunteer prior to them serving is proactive support. I remember one ministry team that I led whose job was to come in and make coffee for those attending church. To support them, I came in earlier and made coffee for them. As a result of this simple act of service, they felt equipped and highly valued in their service to others.

Reactive Support: Be Available to Volunteers in the Work

We all encounter problems we can't solve or face unfamiliar circumstances as we attempt something new. When those things happen to volunteers, they need someone who is available to help them solve the problem or understand the circumstances. It can be you but doesn't always have to be you. The key is having someone available on the volunteer's timetable.

Support means helping your volunteers when you are needed and standing back when you aren't. It's a tricky balance! Don't get in the way of volunteers accomplishing the assignment they have been asked to complete, but be accessible when an unusual request or obstacle comes along. Think of your role as more of a sounding board or a listening ear than a superhero that swoops in to make everything right.

Platform Support: Position Volunteers for Greater Influence

When volunteers show exceptional leadership, commitment, and productivity, give them upfront roles and credit them publicly for a job well done. Platforming them will extend their influence and yours. It will also show others that there is room on the dance floor, so to speak. The need to platform others is especially important in a growing church where you'll need to share the leadership load to remain healthy.

When these three support elements are present, your volunteers will be able to serve people without interruption and with complete confidence. Successful volunteer experiences produce fulfillment, joy, and a great sense of accomplishment, which makes people stick as volunteers.

UTILIZE YOUR VOLUNTEERS

You've spent time getting to know your volunteers so you can select, train, and place them. Now it's time to step back and let them do the job. I know it sounds simple enough. For some pastors and church leaders, however, it is hard to step back and let someone else run with the ball. I'm not certain of all the reasons, but a few are plausible and reasonable:

- The leader has likely been let down or burned in the past.
- The leader may enjoy and gain a great deal of fulfillment from the role.
- There may be an obsessive bent toward perfection.
- The limelight is alluring and has perks that are difficult to give up.

For these reasons, among others, sometimes we fail to utilize our volunteers to the fullest. When (or if) that happens, understand that although some volunteers may tolerate it, their patience will only last so long. High-capacity volunteers won't stick when they aren't trusted to do the job they were asked to do.

Ministry is more than an invitation to "come, join me in the sandbox"; it's more like an invitation that says, "Here, you *own* the sandbox." When you support your volunteers to the level that you give them the sandbox, they feel as if they are genuinely contributing to something significant—*because they are.*

AN EASY WIN

One easy way to support your volunteers and instill confidence in them is by tending to the physical environment where they work. I had the great pleasure of working with a ministry leader (I'll call him Bob) whose church had seen better days.

Frankly, they had let the facility slide just a bit (well, maybe a lot!). They had plenty of space and equipment (tables, chairs, computers, etc.), but nobody was really paying attention to the upkeep and maintenance of them.

Sadly, it was beginning to affect their volunteers fairly negatively. With some quick changes and fixes to physical environment, people started showing up and getting more involved. There was a renewed sense of energy, commitment, and passion toward the church's missional objectives of reaching others and having them get engaged in ministry as well.

The church saw an increase in attendance of over 20 percent in less than 60 days. Why? Small wins! Wins create energy, and energy begets energy. Activity begets activity. And at least for Bob and his volunteers, ministry took on a whole new life when he paid attention to the physical environment where the work was being done. Little things really do impact your volunteers!

Here are a few little ideas you can use that add up to big support for your volunteers:

- Have refreshments in the Sunday school rooms before the teachers arrive
- Update and modernize decor such as color and wall hangings
- Turn the computers on at the check-in terminals before the first volunteer arrives
- Fill the gas tank of the van before it leaves with a load of people
- Keep the rooms clean and safe, and set them up for use
- Arrange and confirm details for a community service project
- Remove clutter
- Eliminate distractions
- Add a coat of fresh paint to worn and tattered hallways
- Fix or remove any broken items

Obviously, the list can go on, but keep in mind that little things compiled become big things. These "little" touches will make a big difference when it comes to supporting your volunteers. When given the proper attention, the environment can encourage people to stay—or stay away.

SUPPORT REINFORCES
THE VALUE OF THE VOLUNTEER

A healthy approach to volunteer support creates trust with volunteers that will not easily be broken. Your volunteers are giving their time—for many the most precious asset they have—because they believe they can make a specific contribution to the church in a way that is significant and meaningful.

Everyone wants to know that the work they do matters. Volunteer work is no different: Your volunteer ministry is the key to your church's overall success. Be sure your volunteers know they are valued for the contributions they make to successful ministry by giving them plenty of support.

Set your volunteers on the path to success by taking care of details, striking the proper balance between involvement and empowerment, and watching for rising stars you can platform for greater influence. Your support will make *the* difference, setting your ministry apart from all others. Support away!

Chapter Seven in Review

Key Ideas

1. Support leads to success, which leads to longevity, and longevity is a telltale sign of the overall health of your ministry to volunteers.

2. If you want to support your volunteers, you need to be available when they need you and in the capacity they need you.

3. Proactive support includes equipping and training so your volunteers are ready to serve.

4. Reactive support is all about being available to solve problems and give advice to specific situations.

5. Platform support invites your volunteer stars to use their influence to take a greater role in ministry.

6. Supporting volunteers means giving them room to work without someone constantly looking over their shoulder or trying to step in on their jobs.

7. If volunteers get lost in the mundane details, you risk losing their interest, focus, and energy, as well as breaking the trust they have in you to help them do the work they are passionate about and interested in being part of.

Discussion Questions

1. What are three things you can do to increase the longevity of the volunteers you presently have engaged in the life of your church?

2. How do you use the three categories of support (proactive, reactive, and platform)?

3. What are some of the situations in which volunteers could get lost in mundane details in your church?

4. In what ways are you available to your volunteers without taking away their autonomy? List a few examples. How has your approach changed over your tenure in ministry?

Chapter Eight

MONITOR: EVALUATE FOR EFFECTIVENESS

C an you imagine how different news reports would be if no one cared about outcomes? Sports news wouldn't reveal final scores. Financial news wouldn't list stock values or earnings statements. Human interest stories wouldn't tell us the happy conclusion. The truth is, outcomes make all the difference.

But in ministry, too often we shy away from outcomes and results because we don't want to seem driven by them. I believe we can successfully monitor outcomes and results without sacrificing the heart of why we are in ministry to begin with. I like to think of monitoring as a caring inspection, just as a shepherd inspects the health of his sheep to know their condition.

WHAT EXACTLY IS MONITORING, ANYHOW?

I'd like to start off by sharing what I mean by monitoring: inspecting outcomes in order to be *relatively* certain that your volunteers' activity and results are congruent with your intent.

Let's face it, numbers matter. They tell a part of our story—part, but not all. If we don't inspect outcomes and record them, we're missing a part of the story. Plus, no one's memory is good enough to remember all the details of the past accurately. We must record and track what we see as we inspect our flock.

I have yet to meet a pastor or church leader who has said yes to ministry in order to look at spreadsheets or to become a data analytics expert. (I'm certain they are out there, I've just not had the pleasure of meeting them.) Life change motivates leaders, as it should. Seeing people step over the line and become followers of Jesus is at the core of their hope and motivation.

Properly understood and utilized numbers can help you in numerous ways: effective planning, decision making, prioritizing, determining, and choosing.

So, what happened? As attendance and budgets of the average church have grown, so has the need to understand, utilize, and even appreciate numbers. Properly understood and utilized numbers can help you in numerous ways: effective planning, decision making, prioritizing, determining, and choosing.

Being proficient with monitoring is, for many, a mystery in ministry. Dealing with numbers can feel like a shell game that, due to guessing wrong, can generate more harm than good.

FOUR AREAS TO MONITOR WITHIN ANY VOLUNTEER MINISTRY

My hope is that you already have a church management system in place to help you manage the data you are collecting about your volunteers throughout the entire process. If you aren't using technology to inform, affirm, validate, and challenge your assumptions about your ministry, you need to get it at the top of your priority list.

Intuition may get you a long way down the trail, but it won't be able to get you all the way to your destination.

Good leaders understand the need for objective data and accurate information in order to make wise, prudent decisions. Have you noticed that obtaining objective data and accurate information is difficult when you reside at the epicenter of volunteer ministry? Getting this critical information will help you to see the forest *and* the trees.

Monitoring well will help you gain a clear and accurate perspective and will give you specific details so you can lead well. Monitoring your volunteers may not be exactly what you thought you signed up for when you accepted your leadership role, but it's something you should get comfortable doing. And the sooner the better.

Here are the four key areas to monitor in your volunteer ministry:

- *Attendance.* "If I signed up, did I show up?" I need to know this week after week for a long period of time. Volunteers can't do ministry if they aren't present. If they aren't consistently present, then something isn't connecting with them or some variable has changed in their lives. It's not about discovering why a person isn't following through as much as looking for a ministry opportunity that may be disguised.
- *Specific names.* Often we know *how many* are in our volunteer ministry but not *specifically who* is in our volunteer ministry. By monitoring names instead of just the number of positions filled, we know who is doing what and where. It's important enough to say again—so here it is: One of the most important fundamental shifts in volunteer ministry that will change your church culture is getting the right people in the right positions at the right time. This

is in stark contrast to simply getting positions filled. By knowing *who,* we can track more reliably and ultimately our overall success will be enhanced.

- *Retention rate.* Retention is about how well and for how long your volunteers stay engaged in a particular ministry. Retention increases with a clear understanding of role, responsibility, and expectations. It's important to know the retention rate in each ministry department. Some attrition is natural and makes sense. For example, parents serving in children's ministry will often move on when their child gets promoted to the next class. That makes sense, and retention rates are often lower in that ministry as a result. Other ministries typically enjoy higher retention rates. It's important to establish a base retention rate and then try to make it better over time.

- *Ministry outcomes.* You've probably heard it before: "What gets measured gets done." I'm not sure who said it, but I have found it to be true. It is important to measure the ministry outcomes that are important to you. You don't have to measure every outcome; it's the intentional outcomes that matter. Doing so will give a sense of health, vitality, and significance to your volunteers. By monitoring well, you'll also know when you've won! There's that energy component again.

By tracking and measuring, we can significantly reduce the risk of volunteers leaving the church over a situation that became a crisis because it went unresolved for too long. Sudden changes should evoke appropriate action. However, without a way to monitor our ministry, the simple, easy issues might be missed and, therefore, never addressed until they become a big issue and much more difficult to handle.

I got a frantic call one day from a very concerned pastor. Attendance had been going up, little by little, month after month, and there was a definite increase in the number of, and participation level by, folks at the church. Yet, over the past 35 to 50 days, there had been a 400-person *decrease* in their attendance.

They were pretty sure they knew why: a well-known ministry had recently opened a new campus in close proximity to them. The migration of the fringe folks had occurred—but this time he was on the losing end. This pastor was concerned and wanted to take an honest look in the mirror to ask some tough questions. He was determined to identify what was lacking in their church. They needed to monitor what was up and determine why a new church could draw so many away so quickly.

They started with their volunteer base, determining to lock them in and help them to be successful. To make a long story short, not only did this church turn the corner, but it is a thriving multisite church in its own right today.

They've regained the loss plus a bunch more, all because they took time to monitor well and therefore become "relatively certain" of the situation. That allowed them to make the necessary adjustments to solidify their

> *Our ability to monitor well gives us a clear advantage when it comes to prioritizing our focus and resources to get the most return for our effort.*

ministry gains and create the type of connections within the congregation that build a strong, stable ministry. Should that situation repeat itself again in the future, they will know exactly what to do.

ACHIEVING THE RIGHT OUTCOMES

Our ability to monitor well gives us a clear advantage when it comes to prioritizing our focus and resources to get the most return for our effort. Monitoring your volunteer ministry is the way to spot-check your efforts and make sure past successes are built upon and expanded. Nothing is better than achieving the intended outcome. Monitoring helps us do so in the quickest manner with the highest efficiency rate.

One church I began working with had reached a point of frustration in ministry. Todd wanted to achieve certain goals, but his volunteer base just simply wasn't as committed as they once were. They weren't working as hard, and they weren't getting the job done.

After some evaluation (some monitoring), we discovered that Todd had lost perspective and got caught up in the task side of ministry. Ministry had lost its savor, and he was merely going through the motions. The volunteers were simply following his lead.

Todd forgot about creating the proper relational environment for tasks to be accomplished. Thankfully, once that error was identified, just a couple of tweaks were needed to focus attention on the environmental factors of value, energy, and alignment.

Todd began, once again, to value people for who they were as much as for what they could do, which was in alignment with his overall purpose and vision for ministry. Soon the ministry was once again thriving and vibrant, headed in the right direction with energy to move it forward.

No one likes to spend time headed in the wrong direction, achieving outcomes that don't truly matter. That's why monitoring is so important. With proper monitoring you can quickly learn what's working and what's not, then make the necessary adjustments to ensure that you are accomplishing what you intended to accomplish.

MONITOR FOR GROWTH AND HEALTH

Many churches today are dealing with a familiar tension: the tension between where they are and where they feel God is calling them. Part of growth is having healthy systems in place that will take you from where you are today to where you want to be tomorrow.

This begs the question: How healthy is your volunteer ministry? Knowing the health of your volunteer ministry doesn't have to be a guessing game. You can and should monitor in a way that creates a "relative certainty" that your intentions are being carried out. When they are, celebrate! When and where they're not, adjust accordingly.

Monitoring the outcomes of your volunteer ministry will ensure that no one is being overlooked or forgotten. It reinforces that people are valued and that they matter. They are too important to leave to chance and intuition.

Watching over the activity in your church and the volunteers involved is a crucial ingredient to creating thriving volunteers. Taking steps to measure just how healthy your community is may lead to a dynamic shift into full-on engagement, discipleship, and lasting life change.

Chapter Eight in Review

Key Ideas

1. Outcomes and results are an important part of every aspect of life—including ministry.

2. Monitoring is about inspecting outcomes to become relatively certain you are heading toward your ministry goals.

3. Just like with any other part of our church, volunteer attendance patterns reflect the health of your volunteers.

4. The key areas to measure in your volunteer ministry are attendance, specific names, retention rate, and ministry outcomes.

5. Monitoring helps you know where you are today and how to get where God wants you to be tomorrow.

Discussion Questions

1. Think about the monitoring systems you have in place. Based on the systems alone, what outcomes are you seeking? Are these outcomes consistent with your mission statement?

2. What is your process for tracking attendance patterns of volunteers?

3. What simple, manageable strategy do you use to measure attendance, specific names, retention rate, and ministry outcomes?

Conclusion

KEY INDICATORS
OF A THRIVING
VOLUNTEER MINISTRY

C reating a thriving volunteer ministry requires a leader who can create a healthy environment and operate effectively within it. The benefits of having these two essential elements working in synergy are worth the effort and will create significant kingdom results in your ministry. Although manifested differently in each church, I've found that all thriving ministries exhibit the following characteristics:

1. *Expansion.* A thriving ministry adds value by meeting needs; therefore, people are drawn to it, causing growth.
2. *Retention.* A thriving ministry connects new people quickly so the relational glue of the New Testament "one another's" can set and bind.
3. *Longevity.* A thriving ministry lasts over the long haul; in fact, there is no better indicator of health than longevity.

While Jesus walked the planet, lots and lots of people came to see what was up regarding Him and His ministry. We read the accounts as they flocked to Him in various settings and for a variety of reasons. Today, people still want to *come and see*. They come to find out about Him at churches of every ilk, size, style, and geography. I wonder how many of those who come to see would also come to serve if, on their initial visit, they were served by one of *your volunteers*.

A FINAL THOUGHT

Ministry is not simple. However, our ministry is clear. First Peter 4:10 says, "God has given each of you a gift from his great variety of spiritual gifts. Use them well to serve one another." People often fail to serve, not because they don't want to serve, but because they feel they have nothing to offer or they have not been offered specific opportunities. So, how do we change that in the church?

Chris has taken the most complicated part of ministry—leading our volunteers—and he's simplified it. He has outlined the skills necessary to transform every aspect of our ministry to volunteers. From youth departments to our small group ministries to children's departments to boards to our outreach and to even our missions programs—Chris's expertise has the potential to make your volunteer ministries thrive.

I especially appreciate his perspective that volunteers are disciples worth our investment of time, energy, and resources. We are called to minister to them and help them grow in their service to God. Before you can help your people find their place in ministry, they have to understand that serving isn't just another way of getting them more involved in a church program. The concept of serving comes straight from God's Word. *Every member is a minister!*

While the value of volunteers cannot be fully calculated, they are a worthwhile investment. We as pastors and church leaders need to make the investment in them to bring the biggest return possible for the kingdom. As we do we give people the opportunity to understand ministry from a biblical perspective and help them find their specific purpose!

I've been in ministry since 1982. I've seen every size and shape of ministry. I get to enjoy serving in one of the largest churches in America. Here's the beauty of *Your Volunteers*: it is 100 percent scalable. Chris's strategies and insights will work as well for a church plant starting out in a living room as they will here at Saddleback with the tens of thousands we have coming each and every week.

So read this book, digest it, and implement what it says. Not only will you be more fulfilled, but so will your volunteers. Together you'll be working for the kingdom, and you will have a thriving ministry.

—STEVE GLADEN,
Pastor of Small Groups at Saddleback Church
Author of *Small Groups with Purpose*
and *Leading Small Groups with Purpose*

ABOUT THE AUTHOR

Chris is passionate about volunteers. His own ministry began when, as a young Christian, he volunteered to serve in the small yet growing church of 30 he attended. During the off hours from his retail management job he cleaned the church, drove the bus on Sunday mornings, and served in other ways when called upon. A year later he was asked to join the church staff. From developing nursery and children's ministries to small groups and multisite ministries to raising funds and relocating sites, Chris has led in a variety of ministry endeavors.

Now a ministry veteran of twenty-eight years, Chris joined the North Coast Church leadership team in 1997. His first assignment was to "create an overflow room that was a reward not a punishment." Instead of an overflow room, Chris developed the first "Video Worship Venue," a preferred worship environment that spawned the modern day multisite ministry movement that has changed the landscape of many churches today.

Chris has also been instrumental in the continued development of North Coast's Sermon-Based Small Group ministry, serving for fifteen years on that team (five as the lead pastor of that ministry). This vital network of home fellowship groups serves more than 80 percent of adult attendees on a weekly basis and is the hub of the ministry at North Coast Church.

Now as the executive director of North Coast Training, he teaches, trains, consults, and coaches ministry teams and individuals from around the country in the areas of small group development, multisite and multivenue ministry, and team leadership development. His passion is to help pastors and church leaders craft strong, stable ministries resulting in increased capacity to further expand their ministry and God's kingdom.

Chris and his wife, Kathy, live in Vista, California, and are the parents of three adult children, Joey, Jenny, and Rachel.

To contact Chris:
chris@northcoastchurch.com

APPENDIX

SYNERGY DIAGRAM

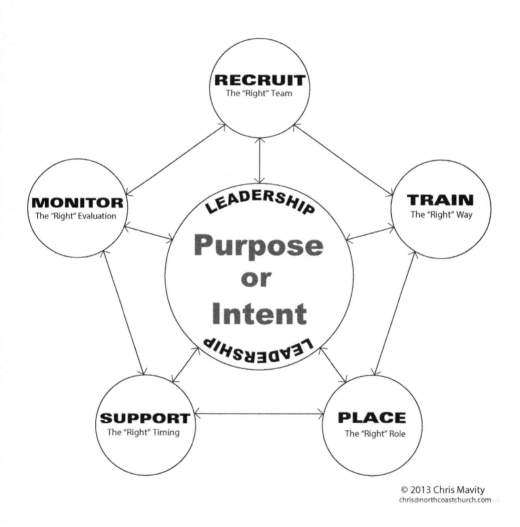

© 2013 Chris Mavity
chris@northcoastchurch.com

WORKSHEET: THRIVING VOLUNTEER TEAMS—ENVIRONMENT

PURPOSE

Briefly State Your Intent

Thriving Volunteer Teams—Environment

STRATEGY

Primary Principles	How We Measure Progress	ACTION STEPS	Who's Responsible	Target Date for Completion or Evaluation
Value				
Energy				
Alignment				

NEXT LEVEL PRIORITY

Need to Do in the **NEXT 6 MONTHS**

Need to Do in the **NEXT MONTH**

97

MINISTRY STRATEGY FOR SKILLS WORKSHEET

Five Operational Skills of Thriving Volunteer Teams

PURPOSE

Briefly State Your Intent

⇩

STRATEGY

	Primary Principles	How We Measure Progress	ACTION STEPS	Who's Responsible	Target Date for Completion or Evaluation
RECRUIT					
TRAIN					
PLACE					
SUPPORT					
MONITOR					

⇩

NEXT LEVEL PRIORITY

Need to Do in the **NEXT 6 MONTHS**

Need to Do in the **NEXT MONTH**

Good Example #1

Dear Sally,

I think North Coast Church has the most awesome youth ministry in San Diego County!

One of the reasons I think so is because we not only have amazing Junior High & High School Ministries, but because the kids in the youth group also serve the members of their own church. Like you.

Thank you for your help with the Special Buddies program. I love how you spend time with Adam Jones, helping him learn about Jesus in ways that he can understand. You truly are the hands and feet of Jesus just by being Adam's helper and friend.

I pray for God's blessing and direction in your life as you make decisions about where to attend college next year. If you need a letter of recommendation, be sure to let me know. It would be my pleasure to write one for you.

Blessed by you,

Mark Matthews

High School Pastor

North Coast Church

Good Example #2

Dear Bob & Joan,

I know you don't like the spotlight. But I was talking with a pastor from another church recently, helping him to develop a small group ministry at his own church, and you two came to mind.

You have led a Growth Group for 18 years, since shortly after you started coming to North Coast. You undoubtedly know the impact your group has had on the marriages and families of those who have been in your group even better than I. But you probably don't get thanked very often for the countless hours you have given to making a comfortable place for young couples to come and get connected with others and study God's Word together.

So I wanted to thank you.

Thank you for using the gifts God has given you, and for being real and authentic with the people in your groups. For 18 years.

God bless you both. You are a real example to our entire staff in your humility and service.

Humbled and blessed,

Mark Johnson

Small Group Pastor

North Coast Church

Good Example #3

Dear George,

That was a crazy day.

No one imagined that we would have 3,000 people come to our community garage sale, or that they would start lining up at 6 a.m. when our gates didn't even open until 8.

But you wore your hat and your sturdy tennies and brought your sunscreen and worked all morning last Saturday. And you did it all with a smile on your face and the joy of the Lord shining in your eyes.

Only God knows the full impact that day had on our neighbors. I saw a dad with his young daughter get a "new" bicycle with pink streamers flying from the handlebars, and even a good, safe bike helmet . . . all for $3. I will never forget the look on her face when she got a birthday present her family would never have been able to afford otherwise. And I'll never forget the look on your face as you helped them load it into their rusty old pick up.

I suspect that little girl's giggles were all the thanks you needed. But I wanted to add my thanks as well, because you blessed *me* with your ministry and service in God's name. You are my hero.

Touched by your servant's heart,

Glen Grant

Outreach Ministry Director

North Coast Church

Bad Example

Dear Jim,

Thank you for helping usher at church. We've been short of help in this ministry all summer since everyone goes on vacation with their families. Could you stay for the late service as well the next three weeks?

Thanks,

Bill Smith

Head Usher

North Coast Church

SCRIPTURES FOR REFLECTION

Serve

> Mark 10:45—"For even the Son of Man did not come to be served, but to serve, and to give his life as a ransom for many."

> Luke 4:8—Jesus answered, "It is written: 'Worship the Lord your God and serve him only.'"

> Luke 22:26—"But you are not to be like that. Instead, the greatest among you should be like the youngest, and the one who rules like the one who serves."

> Romans 7:6—But now, by dying to what once bound us, we have been released from the law so that we serve in the new way of the Spirit, and not in the old way of the written code.

> Romans 12:6–8—We have different gifts, according to the grace given to each of us. If your gift is prophesying, then prophesy in accordance with your faith; if it is serving, then serve; if it is teaching, then teach; if it is to encourage, then give encouragement; if it is giving, then give generously; if it is to lead, do it diligently; if it is to show mercy, do it cheerfully.

> Galatians 5:13—You, my brothers and sisters, were called to be free. But do not use your freedom to indulge the flesh; rather, serve one another humbly in love.

> Ephesians 6:7–8—Serve wholeheartedly, as if you were serving the Lord, not people, because you know that the Lord will reward each one for whatever good they do, whether they are slave or free.

1 Peter 4:10—Each of you should use whatever gift you have received to serve others, as faithful stewards of God's grace in its various forms.

Equip / Train / Teach

Luke 6:40—"The student is not above the teacher, but everyone who is fully trained will be like their teacher."

1 Timothy 4:8—For physical training is of some value, but godliness has value for all things, holding promise for both the present life and the life to come.

2 Timothy 3:16–17—All Scripture is God-breathed and is useful for teaching, rebuking, correcting and training in righteousness, so that the servant of God may be thoroughly equipped for every good work.

Proverbs 4:2—I give you sound learning, so do not forsake my teaching.

Proverbs 9:9—Instruct the wise and they will be wiser still; teach the righteous and they will add to their learning.

Matthew 28:19–20—"Therefore go and make disciples of all nations, baptizing them in the name of the Father and of the Son and of the Holy Spirit, and teaching them to obey everything I have commanded you. And surely I am with you always, to the very end of the age."

Ephesians 4:10–12—He who descended is the very one who ascended higher than all the heavens, in order to fill the whole universe. So Christ himself gave the apostles, the prophets, the evangelists, the pastors and teachers, to equip his people for works of service, so that the body of Christ may be built up.

NEXT STEPS

Use this space to record your thoughts and start laying out a plan for creating a thriving volunteer ministry in your church. Focus on how to apply the principles and practices outlined in this book so your church can begin experiencing these benefits and more: an expanded foundation, momentum that attracts more people, a lightened load for everyone, longevity among volunteers, and a buzz that impacts newcomers.

ABOUT THE CHURCH UNIQUE
INTENTIONAL LEADER SERIES

A note from Will Mancini, author of *Church Unique: How Missional Leaders Cast Vision, Capture Culture and Create Movement*

The Series Originated Unexpectedly

Some things are found along the way, not calculated. Twelve years ago, my call into gospel ministry transitioned from pastoring in a local church to providing vision and strategy coaching for many churches. By God's grace I found unusual favor with a wide variety of pastors in different faith tribes and church models. I never planned to write, but eventually a passion for tool making would develop. Why? I observed firsthand how the right tool, at the right time, can change the trajectory of a church leader's calling. And it all started with the book *Church Unique*.

The Series Is Not for Everyone

Please know that this series is not about minor improvements in your ministry. It's written with a higher aim—changed trajectory. Therefore it carries a bold voice and challenging ideas. It's not written to make you feel good or to entertain. It's not an aggregation of good-idea blog posts. In fact, it's not really written for most church leaders. It's written for the hungry-to-learn leader, the passionate dreamer and the disciplined doer. It's written for the intentional few.

The Series Is a Unique Collection

I grew up with a dad who worked non-stop around the house. He bought only Craftsman tools. I can remember the trademark red color of the Philips screwdrivers and the signature-shape of the chrome wrenches. The reason he bought Craftsman was the lifetime guarantee. The reason I liked them is they felt different in my hand.

So how will the Intentional Leader Series look and feel different? We aim for these features:

- *High transferability through model-transcendent principles.* We are not creating tools to guide the strategy or tactics of one approach. Most books do this even without explicitly acknowledging it. Every book is applicable to any ministry model.
- *Immediate usability on the front line of ministry.* The tools have been refined in real, messy ministry. We will prioritize the application for your leadership huddle or staff meeting.
- *Clarity-first conviction.* This series connects to the foundational work in Church Unique; and each book, while able to stand on its own, will relate to and reference the fundamental tools like the Kingdom Concept and Vision Frame. The books will relate more like engine gears than like distant cousins.
- *To-the-point style.* These aren't gift books or lite e-books created for advertising purposes. We want to bring short reads with sharp insight. We want a tool you can read in an hour, but change your leadership forever.
- *Gospel confidence.* The only real power center for ministry is the gospel, and we are not ashamed of this reality! (See Romans 1:16.) Therefore, no growth technique or creative innovation or smart idea should diminish a gospel-centered outlook on ministry. This series will remind the reader that Jesus is sovereignly building His church (Matthew 16:18).

I hope you enjoy the contents of the series as we strive to bring you tools that are transferable, usable, integrated, and direct. More than this, I hope they challenge your thinking and make you a better leader in your time and your place.

Made in the USA
Monee, IL
21 October 2020